Entering Authorship

WRITE DESIGN & PUBLISH

YOUR OWN DEVOTIONAL JOURNAL

CARLISHA VALERIE SLOAN

Studio Sloan Writing & Publication Design

Copyright © 2024 by Carlisha Valerie Sloan

ALL RIGHT RESERVE.

ISBN: 979-8-218-39013-6

"Scripture quotations are from the ESV® Bible (The Holy Bible, English Standard Version®), © 2001 by Crossway, a publishing ministry of Good News Publishers. Used by permission. All rights reserved. The ESV text may not be quoted in any publication made available to the public by a Creative Commons license. The ESV may not be translated in whole or in part into any other language."

Book Cover Design and Formatting- Carlisha Valerie Sloan of Studio Sloan Writing and Publication Design

This book is dedicated to all my clients who have shown strength and courage in their journey to becoming authors. I wish for God's hand of blessings to be upon you, and work through you as you continue to strive for your version of success.

I am grateful for the opportunity to do what I am passionate about – teaching and designing. Your support allows me to utilize my skills to glorify our Heavenly Father!

Sending blessings to each of you,

Carlisha Valerie Sloan

TABLE OF CONTENTS

INTRODUCTION..8
BENEFITS FOR YOUR AUDIENCE..............9
BENEFITS FOR YOU..10
NOTES FROM THE AUTHOR......................14

SECTION 1- PRE-WRITE.....................16
Part 1: Find Your Audience................................17
Part 2: Gather, Interview, & Research................23
Part 3: Organize & Outline 34

SECTION 2-WRITE..............................40
Introduction to Writing..41
Part 1: Combatting Warfare................................42
Part 2: Writing Templates...................................61
Part 3: Self-editing & Professional editing........... 78
Part 4: Finding Beta-Readers............................,,83

SECTION 3- DESIGN............................88
Part 1: Basic Tips for Book Design......................90
Part 2: Front Book Cover....................................93
Part 3: Interior Book Layout & Design................102
Part 4: Back Cover & Wrap Cover.....................106

Section 4- Publishing..................110

Part 1: ISBN & Copyright......................114
Part 2: Creating a KDP Account.........117
Part 3: Uploading to KDP......................118
Part 4: Ordering Proof Copies............123
part 5: Ordering Author Copies.........125

Section 5- Bonus!.........................128

Part 1: Small Shifts to Promote your Book........129

About Studio Sloan..................136

About the Author, Carlisha Valerie Sloan.............137

INTRODUCTION

In 2021, I wrote, designed, and published my first guided journal called "The Architect and Her Blueprints". It was such an experience to accomplish a goal I'd had for 5 years. Since then, I started my own business servicing other Christians by offering book formatting and layout design services and helping them publish, for many, their very first book. Many of those books have been guided journals and devotionals as well.

A devotional journal can be a valuable companion on your spiritual journey, leading you to profound truths, deep introspection, and personal growth. For many individuals, their devotional journal has been a place to record their feelings, meditations, and intimate prayers, resulting in transformative experiences within themselves and God. The benefits of using a devotional journal are numerous, which is why so many people want to create their own journals to share their spiritual transformation with others.

This book houses the exact steps I take with my clients and provides an essential guide to creating a meaningful devotional journal to help you, your audience, and your clients achieve more profound spiritual growth. With this guide, you'll have access to valuable tools to help you organize your thoughts, conduct thorough research, and even templates to streamline the publishing and distribution process.

BENEFITS FOR YOUR AUDIENCE

First, let's look at the general reasons why devotional journals are just an excellent idea for your audience:

- **Enhanced Self-Reflection**: A devotional journal allows individuals to delve into their thoughts, emotions, and experiences, promoting soul searching and personal growth. For many coaches, leaders and speakers, this is exactly where they need their potential clients to be in order to help them go farther and do more. A devotional journal primes their heart and mind for your messaging.
- **Strengthened Spiritual Connection**: By regularly using a devotional journal, your readers can deepen their connection with the Lord and find peace, guidance, and a sense of purpose.
- **Improved Mental Well-being**: Journaling offers a therapeutic outlet to express thoughts and emotions, reducing stress and anxiety and promoting overall mental well-being.
- **Enhanced Focus and Clarity**: Keeping a devotional journal cultivates discipline and helps individuals gain clarity on their values, goals, and intentions, leading to increased focus in various aspects of life.

BENEFITS FOR YOU

The ability to help others reach higher heights by going to deeper depths is a gift that any leader, speaker, or coach would love to give to their audience. Let's look at some additional benefits of writing a devotional journal:

- **Share your testimony**: *"It has seemed good to me to show the signs and wonders that the Most High God has done for me."-Daniel 4:2 (ESV)*. Christians are commanded to share their testimonies and stories of what God has done for them to bring comfort to others.
- **Teach and encourage others/Provide extra help to your audience**: *"Therefore encourage one another and build one another up, just as you are doing."-1 Thessalonians 5:11*. Many devotions are born from a pain point that one has had to experience but has become victorious over. Many devotionals are birthed by people who want to see others overcome that same obstacle they had as well. This is why we coach, speak, and teach others so they can overcome.
- **Be seen as an expert in your niche and field of expertise**: "Do you see a man skillful in his work? He will stand before kings; he will not stand before obscure men."- Proverbs 22:29. Writing a book of any kind can spotlight your business, and you can become the go-to person depending on how well you connect with your audience. Many "experts" have written books to showcase what they know and the value they provide to their readers. Your devo-

tional journal can be that spotlight for you, and you can also become the go-to person in your niche.
- **Passive income**: "Invest in seven ventures, yes, in eight; you do not know what disaster may come upon the land." – Ecclesiastes 11:2. Money may not be the "only" thing, but it is a good thing to have when you need to live. Books offer another stream of income and an additional product to any business. More importantly, its passive income which means that you write your book once and get paid many times over for years to come.

I explained the most common reasons you may want to write a devotional journal and why your readers want to read one. So now, why do you want to write a devotional journal? Use the following lines to write down your reasons, your why, and explore your path to achieving this goal of authorship.

_____

_____

_____

_____

_____

_____

_____

NOTES FROM THE AUTHOR

You will come across this analogy many times in this book: "Writing a Book is like having a Baby."

Well, much like the excitement and uncertainty that can come with conceiving a child, the conception of a book can evoke similar feelings and experiences. As ideas flow, our hearts race with excitement, yet anxiety can also creep in due to uncertainties. Just like getting pregnant with a baby, getting "pregnant" with a book involves navigating uncertainties while nurturing the exciting ideas until it fully takes shape during the writing stage.

Preparing for the birth of your baby involves getting everything in order. You start making room for the baby and consulting with doctors and nurses on your delivery date. Similarly, preparing for a book launch involves coordinating with designers and editors, beta readers, and your launch team to ensure all aspects of your book launch are properly arranged.

- Next, the birthing process can be challenging and demanding for many parents. Labor pains are real in both physical labor and book labor, as my past clients have experienced spiritual pressure and warfare while preparing for their book launch.
- Lastly, after the birth of your baby, caring for and nurturing the baby is crucial as it must grow and mature and realize its full potential. This, too, mirrors how we must take care of our books to reach their full potential through the process of promoting and marketing.
- This will not be an easy task, but it will be worth going through. I pray that God will bless you to start and finish this process of creating your devotional journal. You will fully give yourself over to this task to write, design, and publish your devotional journal, and it will go out and captivate the audiences God has set aside for you to speak, teach, and love on for such a time as this.

I pray against all distractions that will hinder you from accomplishing the goals and good work God has predestined for you to do (Ephesians 2:10). That you will set your eyes to look straight ahead and you will fix your gaze on the tasks at hand (Proverbs 7:25) to be successful.

Understand this: you will not reap a harvest if you faint before you sow (Gal 6:9). In everything you place your hands to do and fix your mouth to say, you are planting a seed- sowing to reap, but if you give up, there will be no reward or crop growth for you to even gleam from. Give something for God to bless. So, stay with it. Start and finish! Sow and reap, in the name of Jesus. Amen.

SECTION 1

PRE-WRITE

PART 1: FIND YOUR AUDIENCE
PART 2: GATHER, INTERVIEW, & RESEARCH
PART 3: ORGANIZE & OUTLINE

PART 1
FIND YOUR AUDIENCE

Going Beyond the Surface

"Who is the audience for your book?" When I ask my clients this question, I usually get, "Well, everyone! Anyone can read it." But there is a significant problem with this train of thought. Sure, anyone can buy your book, but it's important to identify your authentic audience because what you say, how you say it, and if you say it at all is essential.

Think about this: I don't talk to my husband the way I talk to my kids. I don't talk to my kid's teacher the same way I talk to my friends. For each person and how they operate, my tone of voice changes, and my topic changes to better communicate and connect with the person I am trying to connect with. In the same way, you must identify your authentic audience to have the right tone when you say what you need to say. While it is a noble cause to help everyone, you will ultimately frustrate yourself by trying to include too broad information in your book. And so, by trying to talk to everyone, you connect with no one, and as an author, coach, leader, and speaker, that is the absolute worst-case scenario: you will have no audience. This information, knowing your authentic audience, will also benefit you greatly when the time comes to promote your work.

Finding Your Authentic Audience

Most "find your audience" segments advise considering age, gender, race, hobbies, and interests. While those things are essential consideration factors, finding your audience requires a deeper understanding. Typically, the best audience for your devotional book is an audience that resembles the person you were in the past. These individuals share similar experiences and can relate to the struggles you already overcame.

Let me put this another way: Weight loss programs often employ coaches to assist individuals in their weight loss journey. Why? Because these coaches who have gone through the same process and program earlier are better equipped to relate to current clients and understand their mindset and struggles. Similarly, by portraying the "before and after" version of yourself, you can identify your former self and target individuals who requires your help. Most likely, when you see someone who reminds you of yourself, you become passionate and interested in them enough to encourage them because you know what is at stake if they do not get the encouragement and guidance required to change.

To begin identifying your authentic audience, start with the following exercise. Please add your age, relationship status, and hobbies if you feel they are valuable in zeroing in on your audience and give more understanding to who they are (For example, teenage sex and pregnancy, children's trauma, busy wife and mom). Use the following pages to write down your ideas using the following prompts.

- Recreate your past self. What were your struggles and emotions during the most challenging time of your life? This is your pain point. Think about what false beliefs you held. What did your struggles specifically hold you back from? What addictions did you have, and how were they affecting you, your work, family, and friends? Were you struggling with your faith? What trauma were you working through?

_____

_____

_____

_____

_____

_____

_____

_____

_____

_____

_____

_____

_____

- Now, identify who you are now? What have you overcome? What lessons have you learned? Truths have you come to accept? How has your life changed?

_____
_____
_____
_____
_____
_____
_____
_____
_____
_____
_____
_____
_____

- What have you grown passionate about since this transformation? Who do you often gravitate to when speaking, teaching, or coaching?

_____
_____
_____
_____
_____
_____
_____
_____
_____
_____
_____
_____
_____
_____

Somewhere in there, you have your topic and authentic audience. They are the past you, and you want to teach them how to overcome as you did.

Your authentic audience are people who (list struggle/pain point):

_____

_____

who want to over and become (list transformation):

_____

_____

You may want to work backwards. You may have a devotional journal topic already. This is okay.

Your question is: Who will find value or benefit more from your devotional journal topic?

_____

_____

_____

_____

PART 2
GATHER, INTERVIEW, RESEARCH

Gathering Your Audience Insights

Engaging with your audience can provide valuable insight into their thoughts and opinions. This can help you tailor your writing to connect with them on the topics that matter most. This engagement allows you to add value to their lives through your writing. It can also help promote your book - by covering specific topics that resonate with your readers, you'll have a built-in audience wanting to purchase your devotional journal.

- **Locate your audience**: Spend a few days exploring where your target audience will likely hang out online and in person. Check out Facebook groups and observe the types of conversations that they engage in. Take note of the issues that are important enough for them to engage in.
    - Here is an example: If you want to write a devotional journal for married couples, the best places to hang out are within Facebook groups about marriage. or in person at church attending marriage/family events.
- **Engage with your audience**: If you're part of a Facebook group where your target audience is, if it's allowed per the group's policy, post some questions and observe the responses. Consider asking to connect with individuals who've responded and ask if they would be willing to be interviewed for your upcoming project in a

personal message. Be transparent and disclose that their personal information will not be shared, but you want to hear their opinion on the shared pain point.
- **Create a private Facebook group**: Create a private Facebook group and invite individuals, friends, and family dealing with the pain point you've identified. Clearly state the group's purpose and provide a safe space for them to express their opinions and ask questions. Again, reassure members that their personal information will not be shared. Post questions within the group and observe the responses. You can use the following blank pages to write down any observations you feel are important to know.
- **Utilize other online forums**: Other online forums and social media platforms can be used in the same way to connect with your target audience. Attract them with open-ended questions and stories. Encourage people to express their thoughts and feelings in a safe and supportive environment. Be sure to reply with further questions to reveal more relevant information.
- **Analyze the data**: Look for any patterns, recurring emotions, and any undealt or unhealed trauma related to the shared pain point. Again, you can use the following pages to organize this information.

_____

_____

_____

_____

Most of us can do this because of our status as coaches, leaders, and speakers. Most of us may already have a pool of people to ask questions and engage with. If that's the case, that's wonderful. If you are starting off as a coach, leader, or speaker, this may be slightly harder. In that case, here are some interview ideas and things to remember as you gather and collect information.

Interview Ideas:

The following interview conversations may help you gather the information you need. If you want to ask any additional questions, ensure they are open-ended. Do not show any objection or judgment to their responses. Remember you are only gathering information from them; allow your devotional journal to do the gentle nudges of faith and direction. Lastly, make sure you thank them for any responses they give you.

Your interview can follow the following format. I'll use myself and a compilation of my client's responses as examples on the next page.

ME: "Hello! My name is Carlisha Valerie Sloan. I loved your responses and conversations on my post. I noticed you were going through something similar to what I experienced a few years ago. I am working on a book addressing this, and I wanted your insight. I, too, wanted to write a book but needed to figure out where to start. What is your experience with trying to reach this goal?"

CLIENT: "Hey Carlisha! Yes! I've wanted to become an author for a long time. It feels like all my friends are becoming authors, but when I inquire about information, they don't want to share. It makes me feel alone. Do they not think that I'm good enough to become an author?"

ME: "Oh wow. I'm so sorry to hear that. What kind of support do you think you need?"

CLIENTS: Honestly, right now, I'm just frustrated. I feel like I don't have the time to write, and I feel alone. I don't know what I'm doing, really. I have no idea of the writing and publishing process. But I have some good ideas and I know God will open the doors. I just don't know how."

ME: "Absolutely. So, you don't know anything about the writing and publishing process?"

CLIENTS: " No, nothing. My book is not even done. I have so much to do throughout the day that I don't have time to write..."

ME: What do you think is stopping you from writing?

CLIENTS: It's just life! I put the kids on the school bus and go to work. Then, I come home and help with homework. My husband comes home late, so I cook and put the kids to bed. I also try to stay up to greet him, so he won't come home to a dark and unwelcome home.

So, in this particular back-and-forth. I learn a lot about my potential client and my authentic audience. Many are wives and mothers and are proud of their responsibility for caring for their husbands and children. But this also means they are swamped, and the frustration of balancing a happy home and doing what they believe God told them feels like an unescapable trap.

Two other things that I typically pick up on are that my clients usually feel lonely in their authorship journey despite knowing family and friends who have gone through it already. They need to learn about the publishing process and need more information.

Because of this insight, I was able to craft this very book and create services to help and soothe the pain point of my potential client.

Let's give one more example:

Here's your point of view: you want to write a devotional for your authentic audience: married women whose pain point is having and praying for their unsaved husbands. You have posted about this, shared the staggering statistics, and even shared your personal story online, and you have gotten a few responses from women who have said they struggle with the same thing. You send a private message to them to connect with them more and see the area that they need help in...

> YOU: Hey, Marissa. Thank you for commenting on my post and sharing your information/story/idea. I am working on a project to help married women who are praying for their unsaved husbands, and I would love to gain more insight into your story. Your information will not be shared, and I would like more details to ensure I can help as many people as possible. Is that okay with you?
>
> MARISSA: Absolutely! What kind of project is it?
>
> YOU: It will be a book, but it's too early in the process right now. How did you and your husband meet? How did you end up being married to him?
>
> MARISSA: we were high school sweethearts! I had a crush on him in middle school, and our circle of friends merged when we got to high school. We got to talking, and I thought he was just incredible. We got married a few years after we graduated. We were great. YOU: Aww, how sweet. When did you get saved? How did they happen?
>
> MARRISA: That was a few years later, my grandmother passed away. I was really close to her, and my heart was broken. At that time, I found peace at church and gave my life to Jesus. I tried to take my husband to church, but he wasn't feeling it. He didn't want to dress up to go to church, didn't like the people, and said he didn't understand the Bible. It's been hard because I love him, but I want to serve and honor God. He isn't an evil man, but some of his decisions for our family are hard to accept, too. He is the head of our family, but his perspective is terrible, and some of his ideas don't align with mine anymore. I'm honestly scared right now. I keep praying and praying, but it feels like he gets worse and worse.
>
> YOU: I see, Marissa, I am so sorry to hear that! You are certainly not alone. I have been there...

Now, let's pick out some of the things that Marissa shared:

1. Marissa loves her husband but struggles how to reunite her marriage with her relationship with Jesus.
2. She wants to see him give his life to Christ and go to church- admirable desires.
3. She is frustrated with his faulty ideas and perspective which may be causing her to lose respect for her husband.
4. She feels alone in her situation.
5. She wants to serve God but still honor her husband.

Let's stop here. With the paragraph she sent, you have a lot of information to see where your authentic audience is struggling and in what ways they need help and support- the very job of a devotional journal.

Your interview topic, audience, questions and process may be different, so again, let me remind you:

- Find your authentic audience. Be wherever they are, both online and in person.
- Start a conversation. It's easier when you have also gone through what your audience has gone through and can make a safe connection with them. Otherwise, it may feel like you are prying into their personal life.
- Be transparent in that you are gathering information for your upcoming project. You do not want them to be blind sighted even if you do not use their name and personal information.
-
- Ask open-ended questions. Avoid closed-ended queries or questions that can be answered with "yes" or "no" as much as possible.

- Respond with little to no objections or corrections. Whether you agree with them or not, try to remain neutral and connected with them.
- Be patient. Only some people want to talk about it. Many people may not want to talk about their personal struggles.
- Thank them for their time spent commenting and engaging with you, whatever the capacity is.

If you can't get anyone to engage with you

Due to the unpredictable algorithm on the internet, people may not see any of your posts. Don't feel embarrassed. Remember, you can always call up a friend or family member and ask them questions. Invite them for snacks, sit down, and start a conversation with them. You can also research through Google, look up blog posts and scientific research filled with statistics. If no one engages with you, do not let that stop you. Remember that YOU also have a story to share and gleam from to write the necessary content.

PART 3
ORGANIZE & OUTLINE

Now, let's organize and create an outline that works for you. To be clear, outlines are a preference. I have given you a chart in this book to help you organize some of your gathered information; however, feel free to search for other ways if this outline is not what you need. The best way to write is to find an outline that works for you. Usually, devotional journals have a few of these aspects: a title, a scripture, a passage, a question, and a section to write. Without the lined paper to write, you simply have a devotional, which is fine if that's what you want.

Now that you have all this information, it's time to organize it and create an outline. You can do this in a few ways:

- **Solidify the angle you want to take by understanding what your audience needs**. Does your target audience need comfort, knowledge, and revelation? Whatever they need, make sure you set yourself up to accommodate them before you start writing your passages. Focus on a central theme to help you find your angle. For example, in the last section, I introduced "Marissa," who was the wife of an unsaved man. I could choose an angle that focuses on her or her marriage to her husband.
    - Example: I can write from the angle of supporting wives who have unsaved husbands- how to keep themselves grounded, hopeful, and encouraged through the complications of their marriage through bible scriptures of similar complications,

OR I can come from the angle of teaching wives how to love (respect) their husbands until they are saved, which will then focus on how wives can show love and respect to their husband in spite of their differences. Again, this needs to be figured out before writing.

- **Pick out themes and topics.** After solidifying your angle, write down some topics you want to cover to connect, teach, and encourage your authentic audience. What information are they lacking? What wisdom should they consider?
- **Pick out scriptures and Bible stories that support those topics.** If you find this part difficult, use "Openbible.info" to help. Simply enter your subject and read through the scriptures they provide.
- **Share personal experiences.** Write down other personal stories you would like to share with your authentic audience to help them reconcile the scripture to their own life.
- **List affirmations and prayer points that will be important to include after your passage.** Find scriptures and turn them into prayer points for your readers. Be sure to understand the context of the scriptures to make them a powerful force of faith for your readers.
- **Include questions that your authentic audience may need to reflect on and write down to maximize the encouragement, revelation, and knowledge they need.** Remember, just like the interview process, ask open-ended questions within your devotional journal to lead your readers deeper on their journey to reflection and transformation.

To help, I will give an example on this process using "Marissa" again. If this structure does not work well for you, that's okay. Again, outlines can shift and change for everyone. Find a structure that will help you write smoothly because you will finally start writing your book in the next chapter!

EXAMPLE

Main objective/ Angle for devotional book:	Encouragement and wisdom for Christian women marred to unsaved husbands. How to navigate the differences while respecting their husbands.
Topics and Themes:	Loving God to Love others Strengthen your marriage Submission and respect towards your husband
scriptures and stories	Hebrew 13:4, Ephesians 5:22-33, Proverbs 21:9, Proverbs 14:1, Daniel being a servant to an unsaved King, Abagail's wisdom while being married to Nabal.
Affirmations	• "I am my husbands crown and good thing. Because of Me, He will obtain favor from God. • I will put on a gentle and quiet spirit to be a good example and witness for God to my husband.
Questions to help my authentic audience go deeper	• What voices have told you to give up? How do you combat negative voices when it comes to your marriage? • Since Jesus served those He saved first, how can you serve your husband as an introduction to Christ?

NOW YOUR TURN

Main objective/ Angle for devotional book:	
Topics and Themes:	
scriptures	
Affirmations	
Questions to help my authentic audience go deeper	

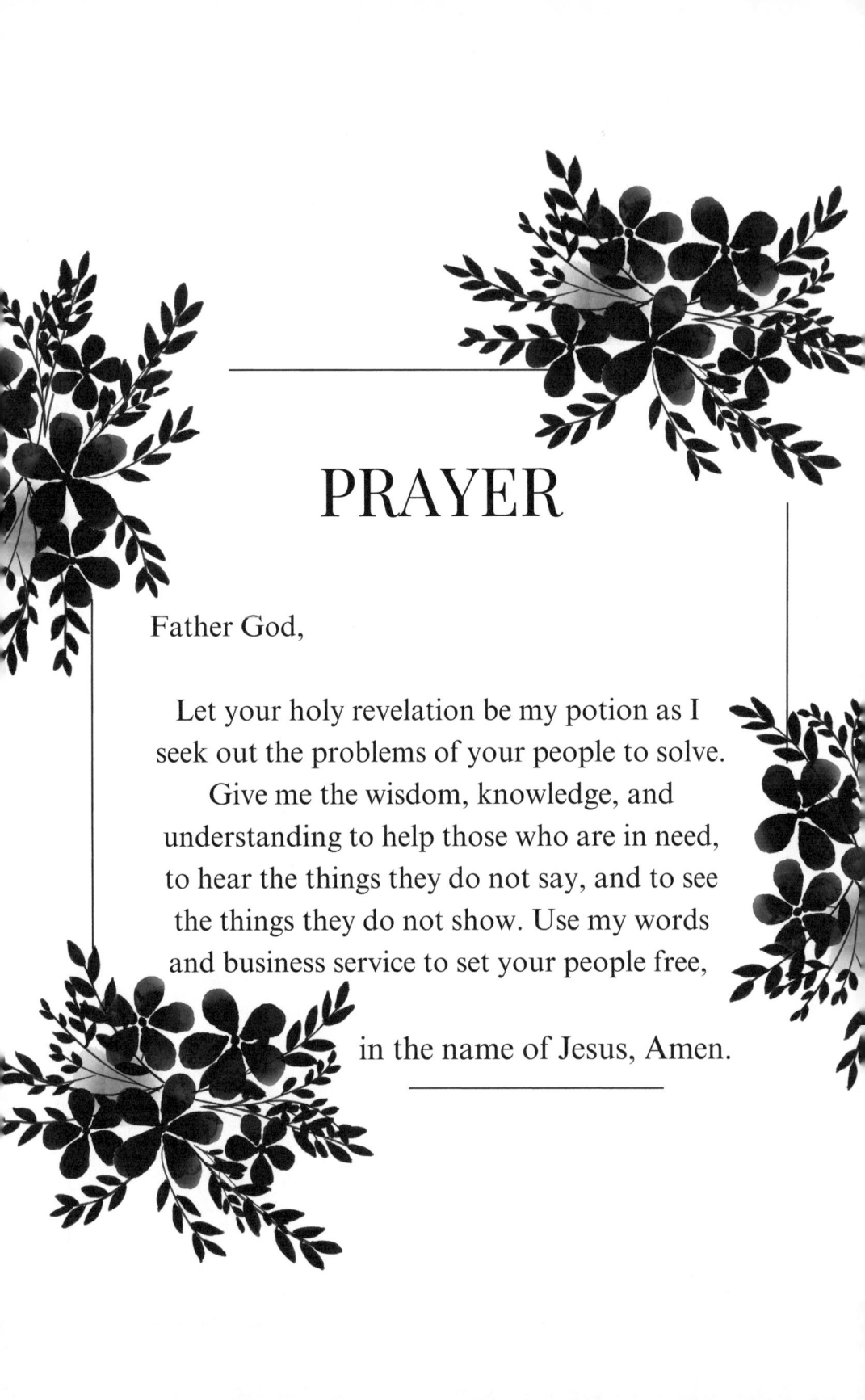

PRAYER

Father God,

Let your holy revelation be my potion as I seek out the problems of your people to solve. Give me the wisdom, knowledge, and understanding to help those who are in need, to hear the things they do not say, and to see the things they do not show. Use my words and business service to set your people free,

in the name of Jesus, Amen.

SECTION 2

WRITE

INTRODUCTION TO WRITING
PART 1: COMBATTING WARFARE
PART 2: WRITING TEMPLATES
PART 3: SELF-EDITING & PROFESSIONAL EDITING
PART 4: FINDING BETA READERS

INTRODUCTION
to Writing

Congratulations on getting through the first section of this book. If you are still with me, I'm sure you have done an excellent job keeping up and working diligently. I also wanted to encourage you: it is okay if you feel you need more time to get your information together. You should spend however long you need in each section before moving to the next. This is not abnormal if you want to move on but feel your book is not ready. Remember, your book is in the newly conceived phase, and things sometimes come together at the editing stage, so keep going and working to the end.

Writing:

In the section, people usually begin to feel the warfare of their project. Things start to happen, distractions rise, and a sense of defeat starts to creep in. I assure you, this, too, is also expected; however, while most give cave in to the pressure, if you push forward, you will find a deep sense of satisfaction within yourself and a massive boost in your faith in God as well because He will be the one to help you through all of this.

Because of all the stress that may come upon you at this time, I wanted to first share ways to combat spiritual and mental warfare and share some tips to help you write more effectively. The second part houses a template to help you write thoroughly. Lastly, the third part is finding beta readers and editing your first draft.

PART 1
COMBATTING WARFARE

In this section, I will discuss how you can get started with your writing without actually writing anything. As the spiritual warfare builds up, you need to be ready. The following are ways to get ahead and fight against anything that may come your way. Some advice is spiritual, while others are very practical. Feel free to mix and match your war strategies to ensure success and victory at the end of this project.

Prayer and Affirmations- Prayer is our communication and connection with God. The breakdown of this act is the breakdown of our relationship with God. Praying over ourselves is an essential practice we must all learn and keep up when putting our hands to any type of work to ensure we bring glory to God and serve His people. As you can see through this book, there are prayers written after each section. Please do not just pray these once; go back and pray them repeatedly.

Affirmations allow us to speak life into our lives and use the authority given to us by Christ Jesus over our enemies and any power of darkness, distractions, and warfare. Many times, as I hosted my writing community, there were talks by my clients about how people would suddenly call them out of the blue as soon as they sat down to write, how children suddenly want attention, sickness comes on them, they experience "writer's block" and the loss of their words. This all happened as soon as a person sat down to prepare themselves to write.

I was not joking when I said that writing brings forth warfare. So, using prayers and faith-based affirmations to combat our enemies, having a clear mind and heart, and decerning what distractions to entertain and ignore are vital. On the following pages, use these scriptures, prayers, and affirmations before each writing session:

"Now in a great house there are not only vessels of gold and silver but also of wood and clay, some for honorable use, some for dishonorable. Therefore, if anyone cleanses himself from what is dishonorable, he will be a vessel for honorable use, set apart as holy, useful to the master of the house, ready for every good work."

2 Timothy 2:20-21

"I humble myself before the Living God as His vessel to write His wisdom and revelation to share and serve others."

"If you love me, you will keep my commandments. And I will ask the Father, and he will give you another Helper, to be with you forever, even the Spirit of truth, whom the world cannot receive, because it neither sees him nor knows him. You know him, for he dwells with you and will be in you."

John 14:15-17

"By the guidance of the Holy Spirit, my words have the power to inspire and bring truth and hope to others."

"Commit your actions to the LORD, and your plans will succeed."

Proverbs 16:3

"Lord, I commit my plans of writing to You. My goals will be my stepping stones and I will be successful."

"He comforts us in all our troubles so that we can comfort others. When they are troubled, we will be able to give them the same comfort God has given us. All praise to God, the Father of our Lord Jesus Christ. God is our merciful Father and the source of all comfort."

2 Corinthians 1:30-4

"God has equipped me with unique stories and talents meant to be shared with the world."

"Don't worry about anything; instead, pray about everything. Tell God what you need, and thank him for all he has done. Then you will experience God's peace, which exceeds anything we can understand. His peace will guard your hearts and minds as you live in Christ Jesus."

Philippians 4:6-7

"I come against the spirit of indecision and confusion while I pen the Words of God. Thank you that Your words are clear to me, and Your peace keeps me, oh Lord!"

"Let your eyes look directly ahead, And let your gaze be fixed straight in front of you. Watch the path of your feet, And all your ways will be established. Do not turn to the right nor to the left; Turn your foot from evil."

Proverbs 4:25-27

"Lord, I thank you that you are destroying the power of any distractions, confusion, and self-doubt sent by my enemy to stall, deter, and frustrate me from completing my writing goals."

Brain Dump: Have you ever felt overwhelmed and found your thoughts are all over the place or you just cannot concentrate on one thing, especially when it comes to writing? A brain dump can be a valuable practice. Before writing, take a sheet of paper out and simply begin to write down all your thoughts. Use no filter, and don't worry about any misspelled words. It may be beneficial if you write it down and then allow yourself to finish thinking about that thought all the way through so that you can move to another thought and do the same until you finally feel yourself think with ease.

Sometimes when we feel overwhelmed, it could be because we feel like we have a lot to do. In this case, it's always a great idea to write a to-do list. If you write your thoughts down, the better you can organize them.

On the next few pages, there are a few pages to Brain Dump. Try it and see how it works for you the next time you feel overwhelmed.

Join a writing community- Joining a writing community is a wonderful way to start and finish your book. A writing community is a group of people who carve out time and gather in person or online to write. Studio Sloan has hosted a few writing communities, which have all been life-changing for many of my clients. Writing can be challenging and unmotivating. Not to mention, it can be an isolating event, but committing yourself to join together with like-minded people working towards the same goal can be the difference between thinking about writing a book and completing your book. For many of my clients, this has been the case.

Here is what Tammy F. says about her experience in the Virtual Writing Group:

"I finished writing my FIRST EVER 21-Day Devotional & Prayer Journal!!! I am SO excited!!!! I am so grateful to have been a part of your writing event. I enjoyed the time of writing together and that we were all pushing through doubt, fear, and insecurities TOGETHER! I loved the PRAYER time and that we were warring together through the attacks of EXTREME fatigue, family things, loss, and EVERYTHING else. Thank you!"

-Tammy F

And Amber B. said:

> "It was a good way to keep me accountable. The experience was pleasant and encouraging, and I got clarity!"
>
> -Amber C. Blakes

Here are a few ways a writing community can help you:

A writing community can help you stay accountable. Many people want to write but need help carving out time and giving themselves quality time to write. Joining a writing community takes all the work in figuring this out. Usually, the group coordinator chooses a day and time for their members to join and write; you just need to make sure you show up. A good writing group keeps tags on everyone and checks in when someone cannot make the group, especially if they have committed themselves to writing. This is excellent motivation; This helps you show up because you know someone is expecting you.

In addition, seeing others progress through their projects and reach their goals can inspire you and help you endure the hard days that sometimes happen.

A writing group helps you receive constructive feedback, ask questions, and receive valuable insight and encouragement as you write. You will likely be writing with people with years of experience in this field who can give you essential information and advice as you go through this process. This can also spark creativity and inspire you; who knows, it may lead to future collaborations and opportunities!

A *Christian* writing group ensures that someone is praying for and with you. As I said at the beginning of this chapter, writing involves lots of warfare. You need like-minded people to pray over you and with you to ensure success. God truly did not make us for this moment to do it alone. Set yourself up with people who will do it with you, and go to the throne of grace and mercy when you need it.

A writing group means you have built-in supporters and people to celebrate with. No one knows the hard work of writing until they have been the ones writing. When you tell someone, "Hey, I wrote a book!" you may get a degree of excitement from others, but you won't get the celebration due to accomplishing such an amazing fleet. No, we don't write to impress others or to get a pat on the back, but isn't it nice to have someone share a victory dance or cheer with you once you have pushed through all your self-doubt, fought against distractions, and completed your first draft? There is nothing like it, and your writing group can help you celebrate properly as you accomplish your goals.

PART 2
WRITING TEMPLATES

Now, that you are prepared to write, lets do it! Picking up your notes from the last chapter, I have included a very simple template to help you farther organize and start writing your book. The first one is a example and then you can insert all your content in the rest of them. If you run out of pages, feel free to use notebook paper and section it out in the same way. The amount of entries is up to you, however I recommend about 50 entries and at least 50 journaling lines.

Things to remember when writing:

- If you are using scripture or quotes, it is very important to write down the scripture and translation you use or the person you are quoting. You will have to make note of this in your copyright section. This is imperative if you are using different translations throughout your book. It is a terrible thing to have to go back after each section is written and have to figure out all the different translations that were being used. Make note of all your references as you go. It will make it easier for you in the long run.

- As you are in the writing phrase, resist the need to edit your work. There is a time for both and the first thing you should focus on is getting everything written down first before you start editing. This is only your first draft which will probably undergo a lot of changes anyways. If you spend time editing your work more than focusing on writing it, you will waste precious time and brain power. You won't have anything to edit unless you write so commit yourself to writing everything that needs to be written first. There will be time to edit soon.

- In each writing session, it is crucial to establish a writing goal as it measures the session's success. In my writing groups, we emphasize setting goals based on an individual's clarity of mind, preparedness, and direction. Most set goals ranging from 500 to 1000 words, and while many meet their targets, some may fall short. If you find yourself falling below your writing goal, be kind to yourself. Writing goals can reflect a person's emotional state or the difficulty of the topic they have to address. Setting goals is essential, and striving to achieve them is important, but if you fall short, instead of beating yourself up about it, analyze the reasons, persevere, and adapt as needed.

- Take breaks- While setting writing goals for each session is beneficial, taking breaks is important if your writing session extends beyond an hour. These breaks help you recharge and may spark fresh inspiration for your next writing session. Remember, the key to writing isn't just about the quantity of your words but the quality of your content. Take breaks as needed, and know when you have written enough for the day.

Title of the Section

scripture

Content/ Devotional/ Lesson

Prayer

Reflective Question

Title of the Section

scripture

Content/ Devotional/ Lesson

Prayer

Reflective Question

Title of the Section

scripture

Content/ Devotional/ Lesson

Prayer

Reflective Question

Title of the Section

scripture

Content/ Devotional/ Lesson

Prayer

Reflective Question

Title of the Section

scripture

Content/ Devotional/ Lesson

Prayer

Reflective Question

Title of the Section

Scripture

Content/ Devotional/ Lesson

Prayer

Reflective Question

Title of the Section

scripture

Content/ Devotional/ Lesson

Prayer

Reflective Question

Title of the Section

scripture

Content/ Devotional/ Lesson

Prayer

Reflective Question

Title of the Section

scripture

Content/ Devotional/ Lesson

Prayer

Reflective Question

Title of the Section

scripture

Content/ Devotional/ Lesson

Prayer

Reflective Question

Title of the Section

Scripture

Content/ Devotional/ Lesson

Prayer

Reflective Question

Title of the Section

scripture

Content/ Devotional/ Lesson

Prayer

Reflective Question

Title of the Section

scripture

Content/ Devotional/ Lesson

Prayer

Reflective Question

Author's Writing Checkbook

The following is a checklist of what you should expect to write in addition to the main content of your book

- ☐ Copyright page (an example of a copyright page is on the following page.
- ☐ Dedication
- ☐ Table of Contents
- ☐ Introduction
- ☐ Before you start (this page is set for anything that you may need to explain or give instruction to your audience).
- ☐ Content
- ☐ Author Bio
- ☐ Author contact
- ☐ Business information
- ☐ Book Cover Description (back cover)

What should be included in your Copyright Page-

I felt like the copyright page needed to have its own explanation. A copyright page is an essential element of a book that provides important information about the legal rights and ownership of the content. Typically found on the back of the title page, a copyright page should include the following key elements:

1. Copyright Notice: This includes the word "Copyright," the symbol ©, the year of first publication, and the name of the copyright owner. For example, "Copyright © 2022 by [Author's Name]."
2. Publication Information: Details such as the publisher's name, the book's edition, and the book's ISBN (International Standard Book Number) should be included.
3. Rights Information: This section can specify what rights are reserved by the copyright holder, such as reproduction, distribution, or adaptation rights.
4. Disclaimer: A statement that clarifies the limitations of liability for the author, publisher, or any contributors.
5. Additional Information: Depending on the book and its requirements, other information such as credits for book cover designer, editor, permissions obtained for quoted material like scriptures, or a statement about the book's printing history may also be included.

PART 4
SELF-EDITING &
PROFESSIONAL EDITING

In this section, we will discuss editing your manuscript. As an author, I encourage you to reframe from ever writing and sending anything without proofreading it first again. This is a great habit to start since you know that your words have power, and this ensures that you mean what you say/type and editing helps others understand what you are saying clearly. To further my point, here is a funny meme I saw scrolling through my social media feed not too long ago:

"Let's Eat Grandma!"
"Let's Eat, Grandma!"
Punctuation Saves Lives.

In a nutshell, editing matters; regardless of how well you think you may write, you must edit your manuscript.

We will take a look at self-editing and professional editing first. Both have pros and cons; however, doing both will set you up for success. Sure, hiring an editor will expand your time frame and cost money, but it is worth it if it means your book will confidently reflect you as an articulate, thoughtful, and detail-oriented writer. On the contrary, having a lot of unedited errors throughout your book will only breed confusion so do your best and be very patient in this season of editing. As I said in the beginning, writing, designing, and publishing a book is similar to conceiving, carrying, and birthing a baby. You have to be patient in all the eras of being pregnant with a book. If you rush a baby's birth prematurely, all kinds of things can go wrong. Similarly, you must take your time preparing your book. It is not a project to be rushed out prematurely. Also, know that no matter what you choose to do, your book may still have some things that need to be corrected. Have grace. Editing aims to catch as many errors as possible and ensure your messaging is intact. You (and your editor) are imperfect, so understand that your product may not be perfect. Even this book will not be free from all editing errors, but minimizing those errors to bring a cohesive product that I am proud to share with others and allow others to understand my message is my goal.

Self-editing

Self-editing means you will be the primary person to alter, change, and shift your book. This can be wonderful if you want complete control over your work, and you don't have to worry about editing that could completely shift your messaging and tone. Here are a few tips to self-edit your book:

Take a step back: It's essential to step back from your manuscript after writing your book because often, we become too familiar with it. We know what we mean and what the next word or sentence is without looking. Because of this, it's hard to properly self-edit your work because you won't see the actual errors in your book. When you take a step back, you can approach it with fresh eyes, and hopefully, that sense of familiarity will fade enough to catch those little mistakes.
Read aloud: Things sound different when it's out in the open. By reading your manuscript aloud, you can catch duplicate words, run-on

sentences, and any grammatical issues you wouldn't have if you were still reading silently. Some word processors and programs offer their platform the ability to read the words aloud for you if necessary.

Ask friends: I encourage all my clients to get someone else to read and review their work. I suggest not just one friend but up to 3 loyal friends or family members who can catch minor to significant mistakes and inconsistencies in your manuscript. These are called beta-readers, which have their section later in this section.

Use a grammar program: It is a glorious time to live with technology that can edit your manuscript for you. Programs like Grammarly can help you spot any grammar corrections that need to be made. If you pay for the service, they will even help you spot plot holes, ask questions you can cover in your manuscript, and make sure the tone of your manuscript is to your liking. Remember, these programs are not perfect, so please prepare to go back and follow the first three suggestions in combination with a grammar program.

Hiring a professional editor

Although self-editing may be reasonable and affordable, try not to skip hiring an editor to polish up your work and make it shine. AI programs that help you catch grammatical errors are not foolproof, and your friends and family members helping you proofread may be overly nice so as to maintain your confidence. An editor can offer a professional, fresh outlook on your work, ask questions, and help you shift and complete ideas more articulately and brilliantly. Hiring an editor can be done in many ways. Simply searching online can lead to many freelance editors who would love to edit your book. You may also ask around or join Facebook groups that cater to authors and inquire about professional editing.

- Here are some things you can consider while you are on the hunt.
- **Determine your editing needs for your book:** When I worked closely with an editor friend, I was shocked at all the different editing she did. I only thought there was proofreading and fixing grammatical mistakes, but there are many more editing types. Here are a few of them:
  - **Developmental editing:** Developmental editing is not typically needed in a devotional journal as it focuses more on a book's plot, characters, and pacing.
  - **Copy editing:** Copy editing strives to correct errors in grammar, punctuation, spelling, style, and continuity of a written work.
  - **Line editing:** Line editing is exactly what it sounds like. Line editors aim to go line by line to improve the quality of your sentences through language, grammar, and structure.

  If you need to know what editing you need for your devotional journal, ask the editor to review your manuscript and determine what editing they think would benefit you.
- **Find and Editor who understands**: It is important to engage an editor who comprehends your genre, language, and the intended message you wish to convey. Editing involves adjusting and refining the text while ensuring clear communication. If the editor fails to grasp your message, collaboration may become challenging.
- **Don't change you:** Lastly, make sure the editor keeps your voice and style of speaking the same. When you write, you will have your own personal style and tone of writing. You will likely use catchphrases, unique words, and greetings and write exactly how you sound. If it is important for you to express yourself throughout your writing, work with your editor to retain that sense of yourself. Remember that you are not just writing for you-

rself but for a whole audience who has their own language and style in communicating, so the ultimate goal here is to retain who you are to communicate with those you are writing for and to. Communicate with your editor on what you are willing to change and what you are not.

The editing process can take a while to get through, but it is a crucial step to ensure value to your readers and build a positive reputation in your niche. By the end of this phase, you want a product you are absolutely proud to display. Do all you can to ensure that your devotional is held in high esteem and properly reflects who you are and who your readers are.

PART 3
FINDING BETA-READERS

A beta reader is a person who reads, critiques, and reviews an author's manuscript before publishing. Beta readers are essential because they are usually the first to give an outside perspective on your written work. You can get a sense of what others are thinking about your book, knowing if it is enjoyable, if your writing makes sense, if it is void of any inconsistencies, and if any grammatical issues are still present.

Beta readers can be people you know and who you don't know. The beauty about finding beta readers that you know is that you know the feedback will be rooted in love and encouragement; however, finding people you don't know may yield a better and more honest review of your work.

To find beta readers, you can:
- Make a social media post asking for specific people who want to give feedback on your upcoming project.
- Ask those you already interviewed for the content.
- Ask a few family members and friends.
- Join Facebook groups that cater to authors.
- Join platforms with beta reader communities like Good Reads and Reddit.

It is important to note that when asking someone to read your book, you must be clear about what you are requesting from them. You want to ensure they keep your manuscript private from others, which includes the title and subtitle. They should not share your information and manuscript with anyone else. You also want to ask them questions like this:
- By only reading the title and subtitle, what do you expect this book to cover:
- How do you feel about the content of the book and the subjects that are covered?
- Are there any areas that were confusing for you?
- Are there any grammatical issues you saw?
- Are there any punctuation issues you saw?
- Are there any sentences in the devotional that did not make sense?
- After reading the devotional Journal, what is your overall impression of the book?
- Would you recommend this book to someone who needs it?
- Is there anything you believe could be added to the book?
- Is there anything that would benefit from being deleted from the book?
- Are there any extra notes or comments you would like to make?

Even though your beta readers do not necessarily have to be within your authentic audience and niche (although it may help), make sure you include who this book is for, why you are writing this devotional, and a timeline on when you expect them to get back to you with their feedback. You want to avoid carrying on this process forever, so be upfront with your beta readers. Let them agree to your terms first before including them in this process with you.

f they reject your terms, especially your time terms, do not hold it against them. Some people are busy and need more time to read your manuscript, which may not work for you. You don't want to expect feedback from someone who cannot give it to you right now. Don't allow the feeling of bitterness or feeling unsupported stop you. Please focus and be thankful to the people who can help you in whatever capacity they can.

By incorporating your beta readers' feedback, suggestions, and corrections, you can heighten the quality of your devotional and increase the chances of connecting with your authentic audience.

PRAYER

Father God,

I ask you, Holy Spirit, to take over my mind and heart and bless the words of my writing. Help me to write what you speak so that Your healing hand will be upon my readers. I declare that every reader will be set free- chains will be broken, hearts will be filled with Your light, the bondage of sin will break, and healing and divine encouragement will be their portion and strength. I commit every word written to bring You glory and honor for your Kingdom.

in the name of Jesus, Amen.

SECTION 3

DESIGN

PART 1: BASICS TIPS FOR BOOK DESIGN
PART 2: FRONT BOOK COVER
PART 3: INTERIOR BOOK LAYOUT & DESIGN
PART 4: BACK COVER & WRAP COVER

Message from the Author: Studio Sloan is founded on book design and creating interior layouts for Christian authors. In 2020, my first book cover was done for one of my writing sisters, who had a small devotional journal she wanted to publish. I didn't ask; she was insistent. There was a lot of trial and errors as I figured out all the ins and outs of book design, but the finished project was rewarding. Hearing her excitement as I transformed her ordinary Word document into a work of art and a ready to upload manuscript was one of my favorite memories in the history of my business. After that, I published my book "The Architect and Her Blueprints" in 2021, which got the attention of many friends, family, and outsiders. Since then, I have created over 40 books with various Christian authors.

In the following pages, I will give you basic book design information. As I write this section, however, I find it hard to simply write a full account of the world of book design since it is so vast, and I am way too close to it. With that being said, if you need more insight or understanding, please email me at StudiosloanWPD@outlook.com. I will be happy to answer any questions you may have.

Formal Disclaimer: As of February 2024, the following information is accurate. Keep in mind that *KDP guidelines are subject to change. If that happens, refer to Kdp.amazon.com as a trustworthy source for designing and publishing your book guidelines. Ensure you review all the details if this information becomes outdated or you cannot find what you need in this section.

The following section gives basic information and things to consider when constructing your book cover, interior, and wrap cover as a paper back cover for KDP.

(*KDP stands for Kindle Direct Publishing, a publishing platform that Amazon owns. For more details, please see Section 4 of this book or go to kdp.amazon.com).

PART 4
BASIC TIPS FOR BOOK DESIGN

They say you can't judge a book by its cover, but this is precisely what happens. How a book looks, and functions determine if a person will pick it up and take it to the counter or virtual cart to purchase and read it.

So, just like all the other sections, this section is important. But, for me, it is the most exciting phase. It is extraordinary to see your book cover for the first time. Things become real; you start imagining your book on the shelves in stores and in the hands of your readers.

The book design process can seem daunting. Only a few know where to start or what to do, and because of this discouragement, many stop here until they can find a professional to help them.

Now, for my overly ambitious audience, I will review some essential book design elements to help you create a compelling book design cover and prepare your entire manuscript for *KDP Amazon upload.

(*KDP stands for Kindle Direct Publishing, a publishing platform that Amazon owns. For more details, please see Section 4 of this book or go to kdp.amazon.com).

Program to use

The program you use to create your book cover and format your interior is entirely up to you. Adobe Photoshop and Affinity Designer are two of the names that I know, but these programs may be too advanced and overwhelming for a beginner. If this is the case, try using Canva and or Microsoft Word. Another program I use is called Atticus, which helps with writing, designing, and formatting your book. Regardless of the program you use, ensure you know how to set the measurements of your document. This will be important in the following section.

Creating the "bones" of your book

Before we talk about any design elements of your book cover, let's talk about the construction of your book.
This will include:
- Book Size
- Book Binding

Book size

A 6x9 inch book is the most popular size for books. However, if you are publishing on Amazon, you have a few more sizes to choose from. Here are some considerations for book sizes by genre:

- Fiction: 5 x 8, 6 x 9
- Children's books: 7.5 x 7.5, 10 x 8
- Non-fiction: 5.5 x 8.5, 6x9, 7 x 10

Personally, whatever size you choose, it's essential that your readers have room to write in your journal. If you are trying to decide, I always tell my clients to go to their local bookstore, Walmart, or Target (or wherever a variety of books are sold), grab a ruler, and head to the book section. Find a book within your genre and study it; measure it, look at the inside, and see its interior layout. Note what you like and what you don't like. This should help you get some ideas and a feel of what you should expect from your book.

Book Binding

Let's first talk about binding, as this will be essential to the overall look of your book. For KDP Amazon, you can choose either a paperback or a hardcover. I'll break down both the pros and cons of each of them.

- **Paperbacks**: Paperback books are the most popular binding. They are usually affordable and more accessible to carry around than hardcover books. However, paperback books are less durable and are subject to damage, tear, bend, and rip.

- **Hardcovers**: Hardcover books are ideal for book collectors or avid readers who prefer sturdy books that are less prone to tearing and bending. Nevertheless, their bulkiness and weight can make them challenging to transport. These advantages contribute to the higher cost of hardcovers.

Having either of these or both depends on the author, so remember who your readers are and what is most likely best for them. Please note, if you are doing both paperback and hardcover, you will have to save you manuscript in two different files because of the size difference.

PART 4
FRONT BOOK COVER

As a book designer, I love to work from the outside in. Even though this is my process, this may be a different process for others, Every book designer will have their own process in what makes sense to them. You will also develop your own process as your work on the design of your book. For me, working from the outside in allows me to make sure everything flows and is cohesive: the outside matches the inside.

Design

There are a lot of elements involved in the design process of a book that we will go over. If it helps, do some research of your genre to see what most books like yours look like. Even though you do not want your book to look the exact same, you do not want it to stick out like a sore thumb on the shelf. Balance is key.

On the next page, you will have the space to answer these questions:

- What is the central theme of my book? Remember the overall and general message you are trying to communicate to your reader.
- Who is my book for? We have answered the question before, but now you see how important it is to get right. This question sets the foundation for everything. If your book is for women, you don't want to make it masculine and vice versa.

What mood/emotion do I want to set for my readers? Colors and imagery set mood and emotions. Do you want it to be bright and whimsical with yellows and blues, dark and mysterious with blacks and deep reds, or romantically charged with apple red shades and pinks? Understanding what mood you are trying to set and the emotions you want your readers to feel will help you decide what colors to use and what imagery to display on your book cover.
- What typography is appropriate for my target audience and an expression of the message? Typography plays a significant role in visibility; choosing the right font style, size, and spacing is essential to contribute to communicating your messaging correctly. Do you want a bold font, script, or something more traditional and easier on the eyes? Whatever font you choose, make sure it appears clear to the eyes.

In addition to these questions, you need to answer, please keep in mind the following:

- **Balancing your design**: Make sure your book cover is balanced, and everything is working in harmony and not clashing with the overall imagery and type.
- **Ask for feedback**: It's always fun to reveal your book cover to people who have supported you. Create a few covers and ask some of your beta readers, friends, and family members about what they think. Gather feedback and shift your design if necessary.
- **See it in the physical**: If you have a printer or have access to one, print out your book cover in the size you want your book to be and see how you like it. If you don't have a printer, you can always create a mockup of your book. Smartmockups.com is an excellent website to find book images and create a mockup for your book.

Color chart-

Colors hold various meanings and can evoke different emotions and associations depending on the context and culture. While colors have positive and desirable meanings, they can also have negative meanings as well. Here are some common interpretations of specific colors. To help with your design process consider the colors and meaning to create a mood for your book:

YELLOW	happiness, positivity, energy, and intellect/ caution or cowardice.	**BLUE**	calmness, stability, trust, and loyalty/sadness or coldness
PURPLE	royalty, luxury, spirituality, and creativity/mystery or magic.	**RED**	passion, love, energy, and power/danger or anger
BLACK	power, elegance, sophistication, and mystery/death or evil	**GREEN**	nature, growth, harmony, and freshness/jealousy or inexperience
WHITE	purity, innocence, cleanliness, and simplicity/sterility or emptiness	**PINK**	femininity, love, sweet, and nurturing/childish and weakness

Fonts-

Fonts are used to display text in a particular typeface, size, weight, and style. They vary from bold, italic, to underlined, from classic like Times New Roman to modern like Arial or Helvetica. The font choice is crucial in conveying the text's tone for your book. Each font can evoke different emotions, impacting readability and visual appeal. Selecting fonts that improve design and readability is essential to effectively communicate with your audience.

TRADITIONAL FONTS (SERIF) Text that have "feet" F	**MODERN TEXT (SAN)** Text that have "No Feet" F
Display Decorative, Eye catching	*Script* Handwriting, cursive

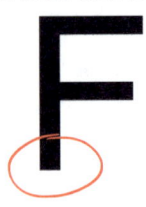

TYPOGRAPHY	WHAT EMOTION OR MOOD?	WHO IS THIS BOOK FOR?	RESEARCH OTHER BOOKS

Use the following pages to sketch out some of your book cover ideas.

PART 4
INTERIOR BOOK LAYOUT AND DESIGN

Now that you have your cover and size, it's time to start with your interior. This includes sizing your interior pages, chapter headings, page numbers, and graphics if you want to include them.

Sizing

First, you must size your interior paper within your program where you are typing and inserting your book content. In your sizing, you must add .25 inches to your interior pages to account for the printer's page stretch requirements.

- Example: If your book is 6x9, you will have to size your interior pages to 6.25x9.25. Your book will still be considered as 6x9 even with the .25 added.

Margins and bleed

If your program allows, make sure you design with the margins visible. If your words go out the borders of your margins, KDP will mark it as an error, and you will only be able to publish your book once this error is fixed.

If you have any images in your book, the "bleed" of your book will allow you to have your images go past the margins and flow through the page.

Here is an example of words going outside the margins.

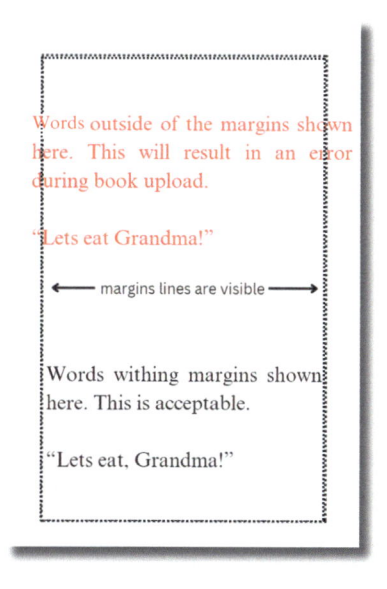

Words outside of the margins shown here. This will result in an error during book upload.

"Lets eat Grandma!"

⟵ margins lines are visible ⟶

Words withing margins shown here. This is acceptable.

"Lets eat, Grandma!"

Here is an example of the two options of "bleed" and "no bleed". You will have this option when you upload your book. This will be covered in the next section.

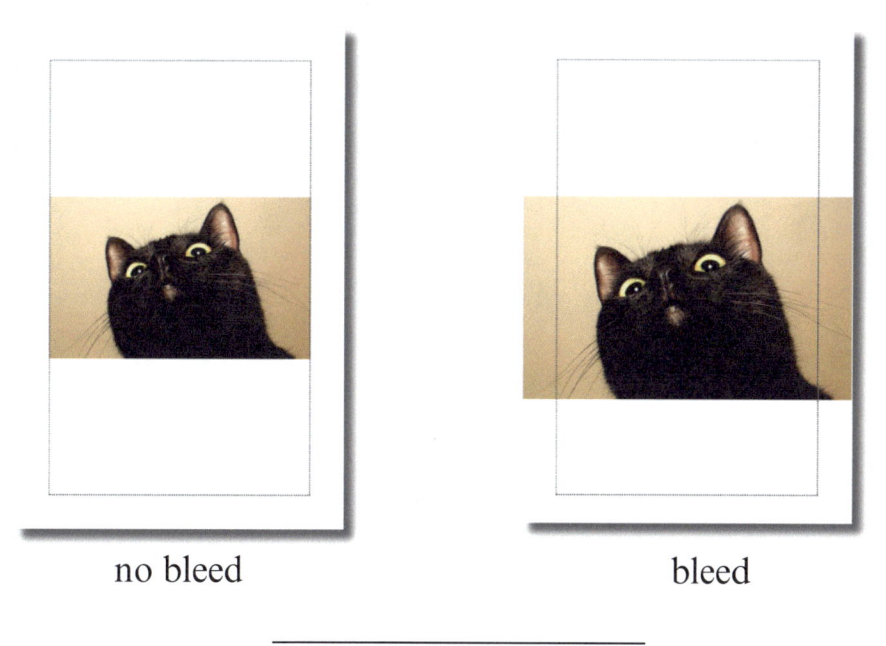

no bleed   bleed

Design

It's essential to have consistency throughout your book, so make sure you incorporate any fonts and images you use within the exterior. Remember, you want to convey a consistent mood and emotion throughout your book.

If you want images, let's say you would like to place an image of a flower within your interior book; I suggest you first place and format your words within the layout, then add any images around your words. Ensure your images do not add too much clutter or obscure words. Words are the most important thing about your book, so you want to make sure your words are legible, and your journal lines are clear for your readers to write.

Black and White or Color

Another thing to consider is if you want your interior to be black and white or in color. Typically, a black-and-white interior costs less than those in color, especially if you have a lot of imagery. Amazon also has an option for premium color if you print in paperback. This ensures vibrancy and color quality throughout your book. However, it comes with a higher cost when printing.

example of black and white:

BENEFITS FOR YOU

The ability to help others reach higher heights by going to deeper depth is a gift that any leader, speaker, or coach would love to give to their audience. Let's look at some additional benefits of writing a devotional journal for you:

- **Share your testimony**: "It has seemed good to me to show the signs and wonders that the Most High God has done for me."-Daniel 4:2 (ESV). Christians are commanded to share their testimonies, or stories of what God has done for them, to comfort others.
- **Teach and encourage others/Provide extra help to your audience**: "Therefore encourage one another and build one another up, just as you are doing."-1 Thessalonians 5:11. Many devotions are born from a pain point that one has had to experience but has become victorious over. Many devotionals are birthed by people who want to see others overcome that same obstacle they had as well. This is why we coach, speak, and teach others so they can overcome, too.
- **Be seen as an expert in your niche and field of expertise**: "Do you see a man skillful in his work? He will stand before kings; he will not stand before obscure men."- Proverbs 22:29. Writing a book of any kind can spotlight your business, and you can become a go-to person depending on how well you connect with your audience. Many "experts" have written books to showcase what they know and the value they provide to their

BENEFITS FOR YOUR AUDIENCE

First, let's look at the general reason why devotional journals are just an excellent idea for your audience.

- **Enhanced Self-Reflection**: A devotional journal allows individuals to delve into their thoughts, emotions, and experiences, promoting soul searching and personal growth. For many coaches, leaders and speakers, this is exactly where they need their potential clients to be in order to help them go farther and do more. A devotional journal primes their heart and mind for your messaging
- **Strengthened Spiritual Connection**: By regularly using a devotional journal, your readers can deepen their connection with the Lord and find peace, guidance, and a sense of purpose.
- **Improved Mental Well-being**: Journaling offers a therapeutic outlet to express thoughts and emotions, reducing stress and anxiety and promoting overall mental well-being.
- **Enhanced Focus and Clarity**: Keeping a devotional journal cultivates discipline and helps individuals gain clarity on their values, goals, and intentions, leading to increased focus in various aspects of life.

example of color:

BENEFITS FOR YOU

The ability to help others reach higher heights by going to deeper depth is a gift that any leader, speaker, or coach would love to give to their audience. Let's look at some additional benefits of writing a devotional journal for you:

- **Share your testimony**: "It has seemed good to me to show the signs and wonders that the Most High God has done for me."-Daniel 4:2 (ESV). Christians are commanded to share their testimonies, or stories of what God has done for them, to comfort others.
- **Teach and encourage others/Provide extra help to your audience**: "Therefore encourage one another and build one another up, just as you are doing."-1 Thessalonians 5:11. Many devotions are born from a pain point that one has had to experience but has become victorious over. Many devotionals are birthed by people who want to see others overcome that same obstacle they had as well. This is why we coach, speak, and teach others so they can overcome, too.
- **Be seen as an expert in your niche and field of expertise**: "Do you see a man skillful in his work? He will stand before kings; he will not stand before obscure men."- Proverbs 22:29. Writing a book of any kind can spotlight your business, and you can become a go-to person depending on how well you connect with your audience. Many "experts" have written books to showcase what they know and the value they provide to their

BENEFITS FOR YOUR AUDIENCE

First, let's look at the general reason why devotional journals are just an excellent idea for your audience.

- **Enhanced Self-Reflection**: A devotional journal allows individuals to delve into their thoughts, emotions, and experiences, promoting soul searching and personal growth. For many coaches, leaders and speakers, this is exactly where they need their potential clients to be in order to help them go farther and do more. A devotional journal primes their heart and mind for your messaging
- **Strengthened Spiritual Connection**: By regularly using a devotional journal, your readers can deepen their connection with the Lord and find peace, guidance, and a sense of purpose.
- **Improved Mental Well-being**: Journaling offers a therapeutic outlet to express thoughts and emotions, reducing stress and anxiety and promoting overall mental well-being.
- **Enhanced Focus and Clarity**: Keeping a devotional journal cultivates discipline and helps individuals gain clarity on their values, goals, and intentions, leading to increased focus in various aspects of life.

PART 4
BACK COVER & WRAP COVER

The back cover is usually the final step in my process, but it holds equal significance. When you flip your book over to read the description, your back cover is the first thing people seek to determine if they should read it. This is my last step because to add your back cover to your spine and front cover, you have to know how many pages your book has to create a wrap cover.

A wrap cover is precisely what it sounds like. The front, spine, and back cover are combined to create one sheet to wrap around the book by a printing service. The easiest way to create a wrap cover is using a KDP template. The following directions will help you create a wrap cover for your book.

Go to **kdp.amazon.com/en US/cover-templates** and fill out the information for your book:
- binding (hardcover/paperback)
- interior type (black and white/premium color/standard color (for paperback binding only)
- paper type (cream paper/white paper)
- paper direction turn (left to right (typical for English language books)/right to left (usually books by in other languages)
- measurement in units (inches
- interior trim size (book size)
- page count. The number of pages you have in your book *after* formatting it to the book size you choose.

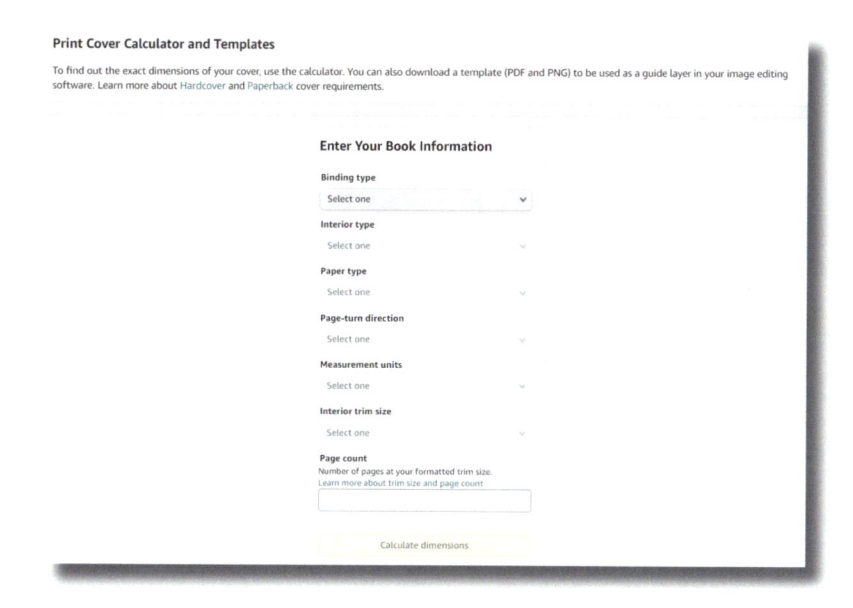

- After filling out all sections, click "Calculate dimensions" at the bottom.

- Another page will open, showing a template form.
- On the top right side of the screen, you will have the dimensions for your wrap cover. The "Full Cover" width and height are the dimensions for your wrap cover (underlined in the bottom picture).
    - In the example. The width is 12.52 and the height is 9.25.
    - Add .25 to both numbers, which will get us 12.77 and 9.50. These are your final measurements.

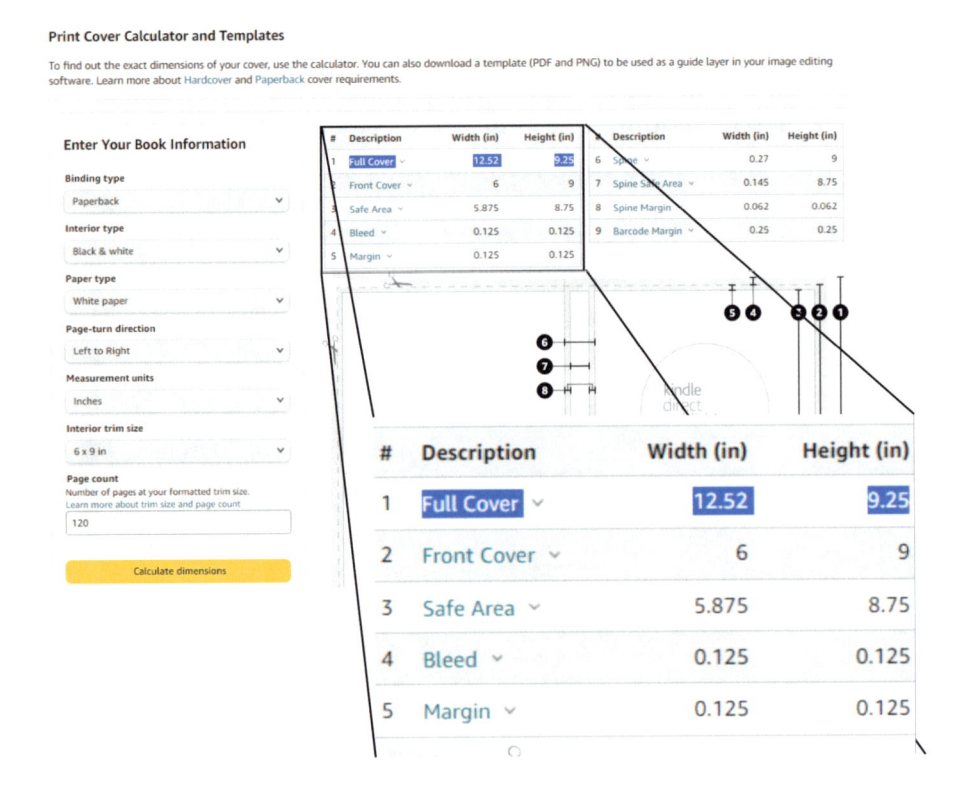

- Go to the lower left side and click on "download template." Save the template to your computer and upload it to the program of your choice.

- Type the final measurements within your program to create a design and insert the template in your program. This is shown below.
    - Make sure your design fits the front, spine, and back cover as you want.

Please note. According to Amazon, you have to have at least 79 pages to have words on your spine to avoid a future kdp error. If you have less than 100 pages, you can have a design on your cover but leave your spine void of words.

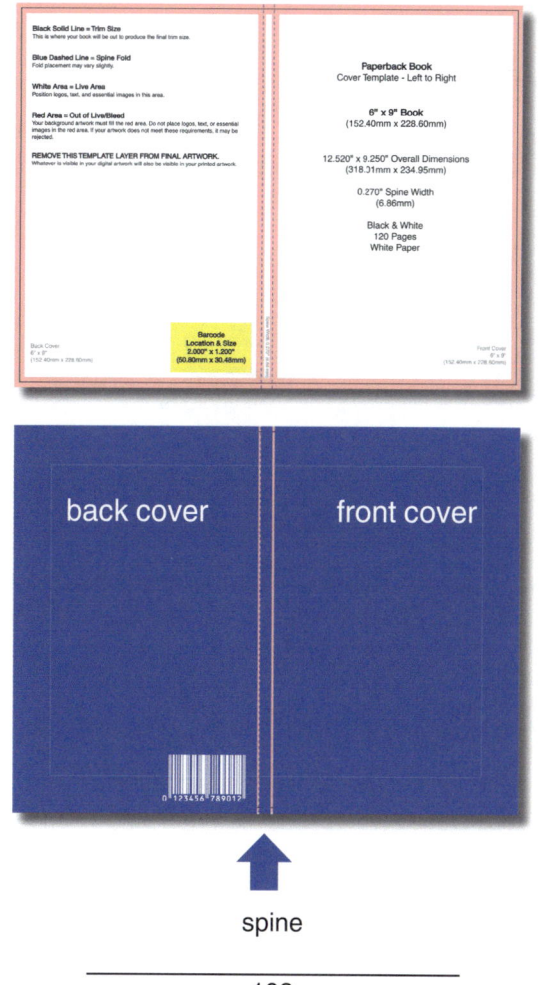

Author's Checkbook

Below is a check list to help you keep track of all the decisions and information that you need to keep track of. Some things were covered in the last section, some will be covered in the upcoming section of the book.

☐ Book Size _____

☐ Binding _____

☐ Black and White or Color _____

☐ White or Cream Page Color _____

☐ Matte or Glossy Cover _____

PRAYER

Father God,

You are the God in which all things flow. You created mountains, lakes, the sky, and the stars with Your mighty words. Lord, I thank you that you have shown me that You are a creative God. I ask you to bless my creativity as I design my book cover. I wait on You to give me supernatural visions and images that will properly captivate the audience you have set aside for me to help.

in the name of Jesus, Amen.

SECTION 4

PUBLISHING

PART 1: ISBN & COPYRIGHT
PART 2: CREATING YOUR KDP ACCOUNT
PART 3: UPLOAD TO AMAZON KDP
PART 4: REQUEST PROOF COPIES
PART 5: ORDERING AUTHOR COPIES

Disclaimer: As of February 2024, the following information is accurate. Keep in mind that *KDP guidelines are subject to change. If that happens, refer to Kdp.amazon.com as a trustworthy source for publishing your book guidelines. Ensure you review all the details if this information becomes outdated or you cannot find what you need in this section.

By February 2024, all ISBN and Copyright information is confirmed to be accurate, per Bowker.com and the U.S. Copyright Office. If you encounter any problems, kindly consult Bowker for ISBN-related queries and the U.S. Copyright Office for copyright concerns in case the information is outdated or not found in the following section.

PART 1
ISBN & COPYRIGHT

An author needs an ISBN to uniquely identify and distribute their book on the market. The ISBN (International Standard Book Number) is a globally unique identifier for books that allows retailers, libraries, and readers to find the book quickly and easily. The ISBN allows your book to be registered in various directories and databases, making it easier to find and sell. The ISBN is also essential for processing orders, managing book inventory, and tracking sales.

There are many avenues you can use to obtain an ISBN; however, I can only personally recommend Bowker.

KDP ISBN

If you opt not to buy an ISBN for your book through Bowker, you can acquire an ISBN from KDP, which Amazon provides for free. However, with this ISBN, you won't be able to sell your book anywhere else, whether online or offline.

If you prefer to wait to purchase your own ISBN, you can use a KDP ISBN in the meantime. However, when you purchase an ISBN for your book, you must remove the old book version that has the ISBN from KDP and re-upload the book with the new ISBN and barcode you purchased. This process will result in losing your reviews on your

Amazon page, even though the book's content remains the same. If you are going through Amazon to receive an ISBN, they will place your barcode on the back of your book, pictured here:

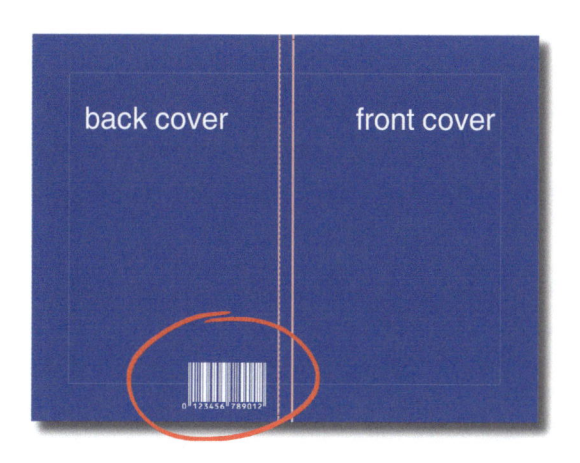

If you purchase your own ISBN and barcode, you may place it on the back wherever you would like; make sure in the Upload section, you click on the appreciate box so that Amazon does not place another barcode on the back of your cover. The upload process will be covered in the next section.

Purchasing different ISBNs

If you have a hardcover, paperback, and eBook for the same book, you will need 3 different ISBN for each book format.

If your book title, subtitle, or any additions or subtractions of your book ever change, this will be considered a new edition, and you must buy another ISBN for your new edition.

Copyright

Buying a copyright for your book is crucial in protecting your devotional journal and having exclusive rights to reproduce and distribute it. Copyright is a form of legal protection given to authors of original works and intellectual creations. When you buy a copyright for your book, you are securing the rights to control how your work is used and preventing others from copying or using it without your permission.

To buy a copyright for your book, you don't have to "purchase" it traditionally. Copyright protection is automatically granted to the work's creator as soon as it is fixed in a tangible form, such as when written down or saved on a computer. However, registering your copyright provides additional benefits, including the ability to sue for infringement and ensuring a public record of your ownership. The process of registering a copyright usually involves: Filling out an application. Paying a fee. Submitting a copy of your work including book cover and content. You can purchase your copyright for your devotional journal at the U.S. Copyright Office online: www.copyright.gov.

PART 2
CREATING YOUR KDP ACCOUNT

Next, we will discuss setting up your KDP account. KDP is the online book distributor for Amazon, the largest book distributor in the world. Some may question why I chose KDP despite reservations from other authors. Personally, I opt for KDP due to its speed and simplicity, especially for newcomers, although there are alternative platforms such as Barnes and Noble and IngramSpark to upload your book. It's possible to upload on another platform alongside Amazon, provided you have purchased an ISBN.

To create a KDP Amazon account, go to kdp.amazon.com (page shown below) and click "Join KDP" at the top. From here, you will answer the personal questions and prompts.

To make a KDP account, you must have the following information:
- Name
- Address
- birthday
- Banking information
- Tax information

To complete this process, you must fill out your banking and tax information to receive your royalties. If you do not fill out this portion, you cannot finish the process of publishing.

PART 3
UPLOAD TO AMAZON KDP

Once you finish creating your account, you can access your portal to keep track and manage your book. To upload your book, sign in to your KDP account and select "Bookshelf," which is found at the top of the page. You should then see the page pictured below.

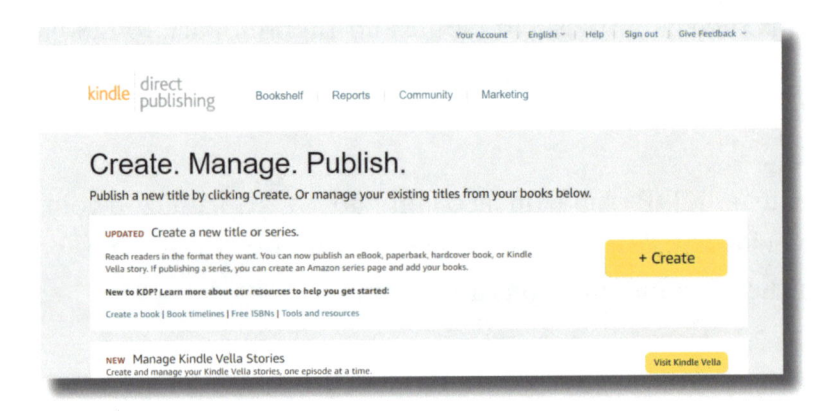

Select "Create" and then click on "Paperback". If you have created a hardcover book or eBook of your book, you will click on the correlating option. You will see three new tabs at the top of your page. Paperback Details Paperback Content Paperback Rights & Pricing.

Paperback Details

The first tab, Paperback Details, consists of the following information. Fill out each section. If I know any extra information that will benefit you, you will find it in parathesis.
- Language
- Book Title (If you have purchased your ISBN, you must enter this information exactly how it was when you bought your ISBN. Otherwise, you will run into errors on the next page).
- Series
- Edition Number
- Author
- Contributors
- Description
- Publishing Right
- Primary Audience
- Primary Marketplace
- Categories
- Keywords
- Publication Date
- Release Date

Once you have filled these categories, you can save and continue to go to the next page. Click "Save and Continue."

Paperback Content

On tab two, Paperback Content, you will continue to fill out each category and upload your files (Note: files must be saved as PDF to be uploaded).

- ISBN (If you would like to use KDP ISBN, make sure the option is chosen, and you then click on the yellow button "Assign me a free KDP ISBN. If you have purchased your own ISBN, make sure this option is selected. Two boxes will come up asking for your ISBN and the Imprint. The Imprint was chosen by you when you purchased your ISBN. If you don't remember your Imprint, go back to where you bought your ISBN, or you can go to isbnsearch.org and insert your ISBN, and it will tell you the Imprint the book is registered under.
- Print Options
- Color
- Trim Size
- Bleed Settings (when in doubt, I always pick "Bleed"; however, you will have to make sure your interior document is saved as a PDF.
- Paperback cover finish
    - Matte or Gloss
- Manuscript (this is where you will upload your saved copy of your interior book ONLY)
- Book Cover (If you created your Cover, click the next option, "Upload a Cover you already have," and upload your PDF wrap cover.

- AI generated Content

- Book Preview (before you can go to the next tab, you must Preview your book. When all previous options are filled out, click "Launch Previewer," which will light up in bright yellow. This action may take up to a few seconds to a few minutes. Be patient. You will then see the layout of your book and book cover. Any errors that need to be corrected will appear on the left-hand side of your screen, along with the page numbers and type of error you have. You will need to correct the errors and upload your manuscript/book cover again before you can move on and approve your book.

Paperback Rights & Pricing

The last tab, Paperback Rights & Pricing, will cover the following categories.
- Territories
- Primary marketplace
- Pricing, Royalties & Distrubutions (This is where you set your book pricing. Please make sure you select the royalty percentage you would like to receive.
- Terms of Conditions
- Request a Book Proof (to order your proof copy, refer to next page).

PART 4
REQUEST PROOF COPIES

Proof copies are available to the author so that they can receive a physical copy of their book and how it will look. The only difference is that there will be a gray line on your cover to prevent the selling of that copy.

To order your proof copy, at the bottom of the "Paperback Rights & Pricing," you can order up to 5 copies. A notification and instructions will pop up. Click "Confirm Proof Request".

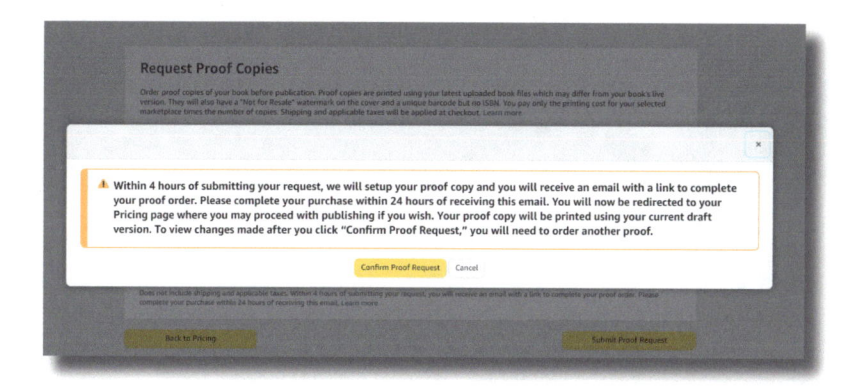

Once you get your email, follow the directions given in the email to complete the transaction. If you miss the 24-hour window to order your proof after the email is sent, you will have to go back in and order again.

After that, save your upload as a draft. You can only publish your book once you receive the copy of your proof copy.

Your proof copy will arrive in the mail. Check and review your book from the front cover, spine, back cover, and the pages within. This is the way people will receive your book. If you need to make any changes, do so before returning to your portal and clicking "Submit for Publishing."

Amazon will then inform you that publishing your work may take up to 72 hours. During this time, Amazon may send you another email informing you if any more corrections need to be made to your book before publishing it. Correct these errors and resubmit your manuscript for publishing.

PART 5
ORDERING AUTHOR COPIES

After your book is approved by Amazon, the will send you an email telling you that your book is now "LIVE,". You may now order Author copies. Author copies are wonderful if you plan on selling your books through your website or attending an event where your readers can purchase them. Go back into your "Bookshelf" and find your book. On the right-hand side, you will find three dots. Click the three dots and select "Order Author Copies." Follow the prompts to complete the transaction. Understand it could take up to 10 days to 2 weeks to receive your author copies, so plan accordingly.

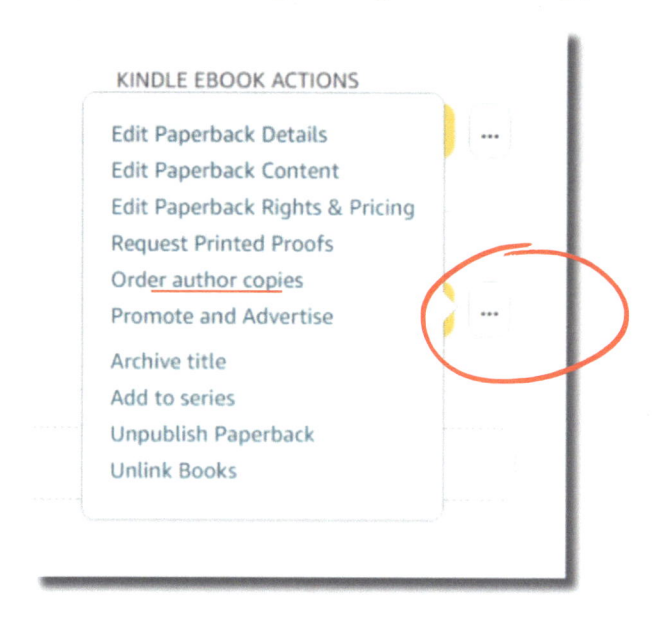

Your proof copy will arrive in the mail. Check and review your book from the front cover, spine, back cover, and the pages within. This is the way people will receive your book. If you need to make any changes, do so before returning to your portal and clicking "Submit for Publishing."

Amazon will then inform you that publishing your work may take up to 72 hours. During this time, Amazon may send you another email informing you if any more corrections need to be made to your book before publishing it. Correct these errors and resubmit your manuscript for publishing.

I highly recommend ordering Author copies to sell to your audience directly. As easy as it is to upload on Amazon, if you sell your books through your own avenues like your website and at public events, you can cut out Amazon's fee and retain more of your royalties. You will also be able to collect new emails and contacts from those buying your book. Anyone can get on Amazon and purchase your book but there is no way of getting to know that customer and no way to contact them. So ordering your author copies and directing people to a landing page or website to collect their information is beneficial all around; for building client relationships, expanding your product line, and expanding your wallet.

PRAYER

Father God,

I thank you for helping me get this far. Because of you, I have accomplished an amazing goal of becoming an author. I know that my journey is not over yet, so please help me to celebrate this accomplishment and sustain me for all that is to come afterwards. I dedicate this book to you, that you will get the glory and honor out of it all. You are my God and I am your child and I praise you.

in the name of Jesus, Amen.

SECTION 5

BONUS CHAPTER!

PART 1: SMALL SHIFTS TO PROMOTE YOUR BOOK

PART 1
SMALL SHIFTS TO PROMOTE YOUR BOOK

Well, you've reached the end of this book, and you should be so proud of yourself. You have completed the writing, designing, and publishing of your devotional journal, and now you're twiddling your fingers on what to do next. I am sure you realized that selling your books can be just as daunting as completing other tasks.

As I mentioned before, writing, designing, and publishing a book is akin to giving birth. After the birth, you must nurture the "baby." This is the moment to promote your book, distribute it widely, refine your message, and enhance your product. Before you do anything else, it's absolutely essential to celebrate your accomplishment! Seriously! People celebrate for various reasons, and this milestone is not one to overlook. Share your book completion on Facebook (tag me so I can see it), and celebrate with your beta readers, friends, and family. Treat yourself to a dinner, host a party, or have a cookout, and don't forget the cake – your "baby" has been born!

Lastly, I would like to offer some tips for further promoting your book. Many individuals become reserved during this period when they should be shouting about their books from the rooftops. I've realized that some people 1. struggle to talk about their book and 2. feel awkward about their achievements. Yes, they feel self-conscious about reaching their goal. Sharing our hard work can be intimidating

Lastly, I would like to offer some tips for further promoting your book. Many individuals become reserved during this period when they should be shouting about their books from the rooftops. I've realized that some people 1. struggle to talk about their book and 2. feel awkward about their achievements. Yes, they feel self-conscious about reaching their goal. Sharing our hard work can be intimidating because we open ourselves up to the possibility of rejection and acceptance. A book is deeply personal, a reflection of our experiences and stories. Our vulnerability is palpable at this stage, but I hope you won't remain silent about sharing what will benefit others and how you found strength in Jesus.

So, without further ado, here are some tips and ways to promote your book and get it into many people's hands.

- **Tell your friends on social media**. These days, you can't do much without social media. After your book goes live, go live on Facebook, Instagram, Twitter, and TikTok to tell your followers and friends your book is out. Tell them how to obtain your book through Amazon, or if you are selling and shipping them yourself, give them the correct information on how they can scoop their copy ASAP!
- **Host a book signing event**. One of the first things I always recommend to my clients is hosting a launch party or book signing, in person and virtually. Spread the news about your book, talk about it, and sign with a smile on your face. You can even have one of your friends interview you about your book, read a passage, or ask an attendee to read their favorite passage.
- **Create a conference around your book**. What better way to promote your book than by creating an entire conference or retreat centered around the message of your book? You can be the keynote speaker and invite other speakers to come and speak on your message as well. Invite vendors, make flyers, advertise, and then sell your books throughout the entire event.
- **Go on a promotional tour**. It seems like everyone has built a platform; find a few to stand on. Book podcasts and interviews before and after your book has launched. You can share more about yourself by creating an author one sheet that explains who you are, what you do, and about your book.

- **Become a local author hero**. Our social and online presence has almost made us forget that we can build an audience locally within our own town and city. Consider calling your local newspaper and ask how you can promote your book. Another idea is to create a postcard and use "Every Door Direct Mail" (EDDM) to promote your book and business.
- **Always have copies of your book wherever you go**. I keep some of the copies of my book in my car. For some reason, even months after launching, I would run into people at Walmart or a family outing wanting a copy or more copies of my book. So always be ready to oblige and receive payment.
- **Have holiday sells**. Don't overlook the opportunity to promote your book during the holiday seasons. For instance, if your book is tailored for mothers, think about showcasing it around Mother's Day. There's always someone looking for a thoughtful gift, and your book could be just what they need. Additionally, running promotions during Black Friday and Christmas can boost your book sales.
- **Work Together with Fellow Authors.** Strength and brilliance are amplified when united. If you have author friends, explore ways to collaborate. Connect with those who have tackled similar topics and explore opportunities for joint projects or events. Find others who have written about the same pain point and find ways how you can work together on a project or event. This not only enhances reader engagement but also introduces you to new audiences through other influencers. Don't be intimidated and don't be jealous of someone else's platform either. That is an

emotion from our enemy, and it is not something you should engage in. Focus on this instead: By combining voices, you can create a harmonious chorus that resonates with your message and guides others towards wisdom and transformation.

- **Keep promoting!** The biggest mistake I see in some of my clients is that they promote their book and message for only a season and then stop after 6 months. One thing I want you to remember is to always believe in your message enough to tell someone about it. I am not encouraging you to oversell your book (every time you talk to someone or post on social media you are asking them to buy your book), what I am saying is to find creative ideas to promote the message of your book. Go out and use what God has given you to serve and help others by the leading of the Holy Spirit.

Conclusion

We have journeyed far in this book. Writing is indeed a path filled with twists and turns, yet, as I mentioned at the start, it is rewarding to be used by God in this way. I want to personally congratulate you on beginning and completing your book and the dedication you have shown. I envision meeting you one day, signing the book you have created while reading this. I hope to witness your joy as you see how far God has brought you! Thank you for having faith in me to impart all that I know. If you have any questions, please don't hesitate to reach out at StudiosloanWPD@outlook.com. I would be delighted to assist you in your journey to success. Blessings to you and your loved ones.

Carlisha Valerie Sloan

PRAYER

Father God,

Please help me to find ways to be a blessing to someone by promoting my book. Help me to lean into your wisdom and guidance to market it to people who really needs me. Help me not to faint before I reap.

in the name of Jesus, Amen.

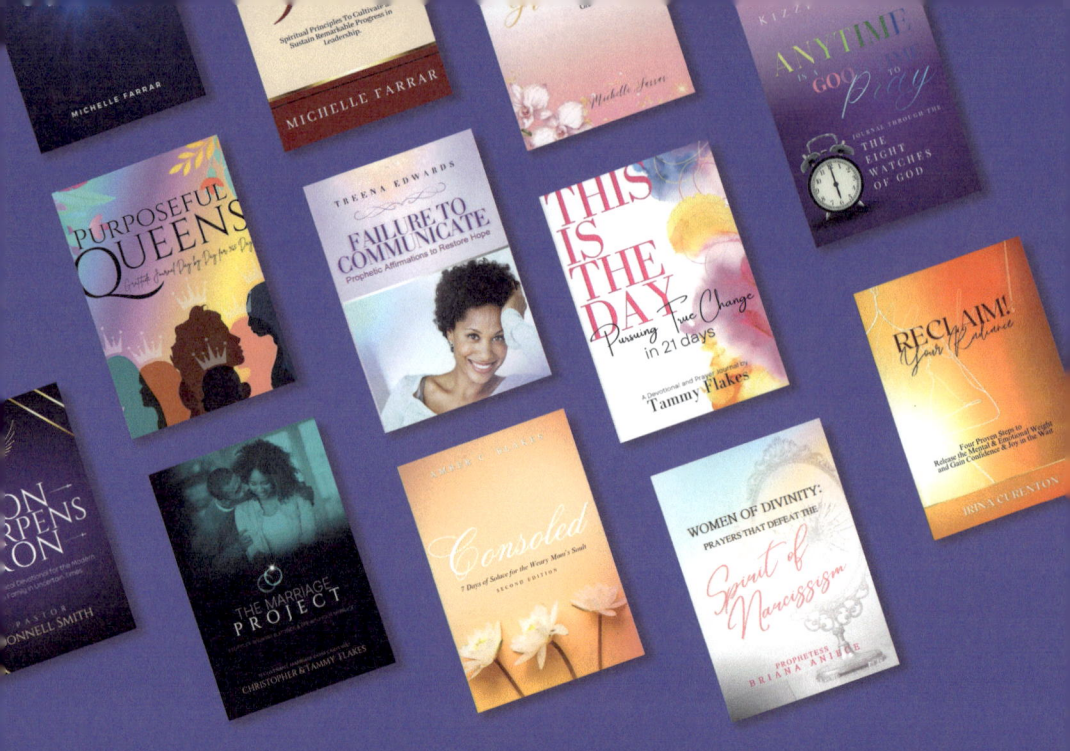

studioSLOAN
WRITING & PUBLICATION DESIGN

Studio Sloan offers creative and essential services in literary design for Christian writers, entrepreneurs, and coaches to prepare their written work to be shared with the masses!

WE DO THIS BY PROVIDING SERVICES:

- Hosting Writing Communities
- Book Cover Design
- Interior layout and formatting design
- Basic Proofreading
- KDP upload

STUDIOSLOANWPD@OUTLOOK.COM

ABOUT THE AUTHOR
Carlisha Valerie Sloan

"Wife, mom, writer, minister, designer, and entrepreneur. Carlisha's life mission is to write, speak, and create spaces for Christian women to become powerful, confident, and influential vessels for the glory of God. She lives with her family on the coast of NC.

After years of envisioning myself as an author, I finally transformed my aspiration into reality. By participating in a 21-day writing community, I received the necessary support to create my debut book, "The Architect and Her Blueprints". However, as a new author, I had trouble gathering enough money to get my book published.

During a powerful prayer session, I received a message from the Holy Spirit. Rather than promising financial assistance, He offered to guide me in the process of publishing books and helping others do the same. Initially, I struggled to discern the Holy Spirit's voice, but as I began aligning my intentions with His, I unearthed a newfound joy in serving others.

Today, I am proud to help Christian leaders, writers, and entrepreneurs in crafting, designing, and publishing content that uplifts their audience and positively impacts the world. I urge everyone to take the courageous leap into authorship and harness the influence of words to bring forth life, wisdom, and divine insight to their readers.

Connect with me!

Carlisha Valerie Sloan

StudioSloanWPD@outlook.com

Made in the USA
Columbia, SC
15 March 2024